# Contents

Introduction

# Introduction

The subject of pensions and the provision of pensions has been a hotly debated topic over the last decade. The issue of catering for future needs has been a problem that has vexed government, employers and individuals.

This book takes a look at the issues surrounding pensions and also discusses the different areas of provision, from the state pension to personal pensions and also the tax and benefits implications.

One thing is for sure, if a person does not, either through an occupational scheme or through some other type of personal pension plan, ensure that they are saving regularly to provide a decent level of pension for their retirement, then they will find themselves, as millions have, in a poverty trap.

The whole thrust of this book is to help individuals understand the pensions system in the United Kingdom, to open eyes to the implications of not providing for retirement and to point the way to the right sort of plan for them.

The book is split into different sections, pensions generally, sources of pensions, occupational pensions, stakeholder pensions and other forms of savings. At the very least, the information contained within should enable a person to make an informed choice and to begin to provide security for the future.

Patrick Grant 2011

# 1

# Pensions and Planning for the Future

## Planning for the future

The main principle with all pension provision is that the sooner you start saving money in a pension plan the more that you will have at retirement. The later that you leave it the less you will have or the more expensive that it will be to create a fund adequate enough for your needs.

In order to gauge your retirement needs, you will need to have a clear idea of your lifestyle, or potential lifestyle in retirement. This is not something that you can plan, or want to plan, at a younger age but the main factor is that the more that you have the easier life will be. There are two main factors which currently underpin retirement:

- Improved health and longevity-we are living longer and we have better health so therefore we are more active

- People are better off-improved state and company pensions

## Sources of pension and other retirement income

Government statistics indicate that there is a huge gap between the poorest and richest pensioners in the United Kingdom. No surprise there. The difference between the richest fifth of single pensioners and the poorest fifth is about £400 per week. The riches and poorest couples is £719. The poorest fifth of pensioners in the UK are reliant mainly on state benefits whilst the wealthier groups have occupational incomes and also personal investment incomes. The tables below indicates the disparity between the riches and poorest socio-economic groups:

## TYPE OF PENSIONER HOUSEHOLD

Income per week Single      Couple

| Poorest | Next 5th | Middle 5th | Next 5th | Richest 5th | Poorest 5th | Next 5th | Middle 5th | Next 5th | Richest 5th |
|---|---|---|---|---|---|---|---|---|---|
| | | | | £533 | | | | | £1252 |
| | | | £278 | | | | | £579 | |
| | | £216 | | | | | £421 | | |
| | £185 | | | | | £320 | | | |
| £136 | | | | | £225 | | | | |

Poorest  Next 5th  Middle 5th  Next 5th  Richest 5th  Poorest 5th  Next 5th  Middle 5th  Next 5th  Richest 5th

Source: The Pensioners Income Series 2008-2009.

## Income sources of poorest and richest pensioners

| **Poorest** | **Richest** |
|---|---|
| Occupational Pensions 12% | Occupational pensions 27% |
| Personal Pensions  3% | Personal Pensions 5% |
| Investment income 4% | Investment income 18% |
| Earnings 7% | Earnings 35% |
| Other 0% | Other 1% |
| Benefit Income 73% | Benefit Income 13% |

Source: The Pensioners Income Series 2008-2009

The above illustrates that those in the poorest and wealthiest bands have a wide gap in income, in particular in the areas of earnings and investments. The richest have managed to ensure that there is enough money in the pot to cater for retirement. Those in the lower income bands rely heavily on state pensions and other benefits.

When attempting to forecast for future pension needs, there are a number of factors which need to be taken into account:

- Your income needs in retirement and how much of that income you can expect to derive from state pensions
- How much pension that any savings you have will produce

- How long you have to save for

- Projected inflation

## 1. Income needs in retirement

This is very much a personal decision and will be influenced by a number of factors, such as ongoing housing costs, care costs, projected lifestyle etc. The main factor is that you have enough to live on comfortably. In retirement you will probably take more holidays and want to enjoy your free time. This costs money so your future planning should take into account all your projected needs and costs. The next chapter includes a few calculations about future needs. When calculating future needs, all sources of income should be taken into account.

## 2. What period to save over

The obvious fact is that, the longer period that you save over the more you will build up and hence the more that you will have in retirement. As time goes on savings are compounded and the value of the pot goes up. One thing is for certain and that is if you leave it too late then you will have to put away a large slice of your income to produce a decent pension. If you plan to retire at an early age then you will need to save more to produce the same benefits. We will discuss saving arrangements further on in this book.

## 3. Inflation

As prices rise, so your money buys you less. This is the main effect of inflation and to maintain the same level of spending power you will need to save more as time goes on. Many forms of retirement plans will include a calculation for inflation. Currently, inflation is at a reasonable level, 2.75% per annum. However, history shows that the effects of inflation can be corrosive, having risen above 25% per annum in the past. Hopefully, this is now under control

************

# 2

# How Much Income is needed in Retirement-Planning Ahead

For most people, retirement is a substantial part of life, probably lasting a couple of decades or more. It follows that ensuring your financial security in retirement requires some forward planning. Developing a plan calls for a general review of your current finances and careful consideration of how you can build up your savings to generate the retirement income that you need.

There are five distinct stages to planning your retirement which are summarised below.

Stage 1-this involves checking first that other aspects of your basic finances are in good shape. Planning for retirement generally means locking away your money for a long time. Once invested it is usually impossible to get pension savings back early, even if in an emergency. It is therefore essential that you have other more accessible savings available for emergencies and that you do not have any problem debts that could tip you into a financial crisis. You must then weigh up saving for retirement against other goals that are more pressing, such as making sure that your household would be financially secure if you were unable to work because of illness or the main breadwinner dies.

Stage 2-You need to decide how much income you might need when you retire. There is a table below which might help you in calculating this.

Stage 3- Check how much pension that you have built up so far.

Stage 4-Compare your amount form stage 3 with your target income from stage 2.

Stage 5-Review your progress once a year and/or if your circumstances change.

It is a fact that many people need far less in retirement than when actively working. The expenses that exist when working, such as mortgage payments, children and work related expenses do not exist when retired. The average household between 30-49 spends £473 per week and £416 between 50-64. This drops to £263 per week between 65 to 74 and even lower in later retirement (Family Expenditure Survey 2000-1).

However, as might be expected, expenditure on health care increases correspondingly with age. Whilst the state may help with some costs the individual still has to bear a high proportion of expenditure on health related items.

When calculating how much money you will need in retirement, it is useful to use a table in order to list your anticipated expenses as follows:

1. **Everyday needs**

| Item Total | Annual |
|---|---|
| | £ |
| Food and other | |
| Leisure (newspapers etc) | |

| Pets | |
|---|---|
| Clothes | |
| Other household items | |
| Gardening | |
| General expenses | |

## Home expenses

| Mortgage/rent | |
|---|---|
| Service charges/repairs | |
| Insurance | |
| Council tax | |
| Water and other utilities | |
| Telephone | |
| TV licence other charges (satellite) | |
| Other expenses (home help) | |

## Leisure and general entertainment

| Hobbies | |
|---|---|
| Eating out | |
| Cinema/theatre | |
| Holidays | |
| Other luxuries (smoking/drinking | |

## Transport

| Car expenses | |
|---|---|
| Car hire | |

| Petrol etc | |
|---|---|
| Bus/train fares | |

## Health

| Dental charges | |
|---|---|
| Optical expenses | |
| Medical insurance | |
| Care insurance | |
| Other health related expenses | |

## Anniversaries/birthdays etc

| Children/grandchildren | |
|---|---|
| Relatives other than children | |
| Christmas | |
| Charitable donations | |
| Other expenses | |

## Savings and loans

| General savings | |
|---|---|
| Saving for later retirement | |
| Other savings | |
| Loan repayments | |

## Other

| | |
|---|---|
| | |

The above should give you an idea of the amounts that you will need per annum to live well. Obviously, you should plan for a monthly income that will meet those needs. You should also take account of income tax on your retirement incomes.

## The impact of inflation

When you are planning for many years ahead, it is essential to take account of the effects of inflation. Currently, in 2011, we are in a period of high inflation, largely due to sky high oil prices. As prices rise over the years, the money we will have will buy less and less. For example, in the extreme case, if prices double then a fixed amount of money will buy only half as much. The higher the rate of inflation,. The more you have to save to reach your income target.

Some pension schemes give you automatic protection against inflation, but many don't and it is largely up to you to decide what protection to build into your planning. The first step is to be aware what effect inflation might have. Fortunately, pension statements and projections these days must all be adjusted for inflation so that figures you are given are expressed in today's money. This gives you an idea of the standard of living you might expect and helps you assess the amount that you need to save.

Providers of non-pension investments (such as unit trusts and investment trusts (see later chapters) do not have to give you statements and projections adjusted for inflation. If you use these other investments for your retirement then you will have to make your own adjustments. You can do this using the table below.

Value in today's money of £1,000 you receive in the future

## Average rate of inflation

| Number of years until you receive the money | 2.5% a year | 5% a year | 7.5% a year | 10% a year |
|---|---|---|---|---|
| 5 | £884 | £784 | £697 | £621 |
| 10 | £781 | £614 | £485 | £386 |
| 15 | £690 | £481 | £338 | £239 |
| 20 | £610 | £377 | £235 | £149 |
| 25 | £539 | £295 | £164 | £92 |
| 30 | £477 | £231 | £114 | £57 |
| 35 | £421 | £181 | £80 | £36 |
| 40 | £372 | £142 | £55 | £22 |
| 45 | £329 | £111 | £39 | £14 |
| 50 | £291 | £87 | £39 | £9 |
| | | | | |

The above should be a good guide. If you require more detailed forecasting you can go to www.statistics.gov.uk/plc

# 3

# Sources Of Pension Savings- Options for Retirement

---

## 1. The state pension

We will be elaborating on the state pension further in chapter 5. The state pension system is based on contributions, the payments made by an individual today funds today's pension payments and for those who are young the future contributions will foot their pension bill. Therefore, the state pension system is not a savings scheme it is a pay-as-you-go system.

Pensions are a major area of government spending and are becoming more and more so. Protecting pensions against inflationary increases have put pressure on respective governments, along with the introduction of a second tier-pension, the state second pension (S2P). This replaced SERPS. The problems of pension provision are set to increase with the numbers of older people outnumbering those in active work, leading to an imbalance in provision. The biggest dilemma facing the government, and future governments, is the problem of convincing people to save for their pensions, therefore taking some of the burden off the state.

Those most at risk in terms of retirement poverty are the lower earners, who quite often do not build up enough contributions to gain a state pension, those who contribute to a state pension but cannot save enough to contribute to a private scheme and disabled people who cannot work or carers who also cannot work. The above is not an exclusive list. The government has recognised the difficulties faced by these groups and have introduced the state second pension and pension credits.

## Pension credits

Pension credits began life in October 2003. The credit is designed to top up the resources of pensioners whose income is low. The pension credit has two components: a guarantee credit and a saving credit. The guarantee credit is available to anyone over a qualifying age (equal to women's state pension age-see further on) whose income is less than a set amount called the minimum guarantee. The guarantee will bring income up to £132.60 for a single person and £202.40 for a couple (including same sex couples) (2010-2011). The minimum guarantee is higher for certain categories of disabled people and carers.

## The savings credit

Pension credit also has an inbuilt incentive scheme called a savings credit which encourages people to save for their retirement.

The rules are complicated. If a person is aged 65 or over they can claim a credit of 60pence for each £1 of income that they have between two thresholds. The lower threshold is the maximum basic state pension. This is £98.40 per week for a single person and £157.25 for a couple. The upper threshold is the minimum guarantee stated above (£132.60 single and £202.40 couple). This gives a maximum savings threshold of £20.52 single and £27.09 couple (2010-11). Savings credit is reduced by 40p for each £1 of income above the minimum guarantee.

## The over 80 pension

This is a non-contributory pension for people aged 80 or over with little or no state pension. If you are 80 or over, not getting or getting a reduced state pension because you have not paid enough National Insurance contributions (NI) and are currently living in England, Scotland or Wales and have been doing so for a total of 10 years or more in any continuous period of 20 years before or after your 80th birthday, you could claim the over 80 pension. The maximum amount of the over 80 state pension that you can get is 60% of the full state pension.

## 2. Personal Pension Arrangements

### Occupational pensions

We discuss occupational pension schemes in more depth later in this book. Briefly, occupational pension schemes are a very important source of income. They are also one of the best ways to pay into a pension scheme as the employer has to contribute a significant amount to the pot. Over the years the amounts paid into occupational pension schemes has increased significantly. Although there have been a number of incidences of occupational schemes being wound up this is relatively small and they remain a key source of retirement income.

### Stakeholder schemes

Stakeholder pension schemes are designed for those people who do not have an employer, or have an employer who does not have an occupational scheme. They therefore cannot pay into an occupational scheme. If an employer does not offer an occupational scheme (many small employers are exempt) they have to arrange access to a stakeholder scheme. Employees do not have to join an occupational scheme offered by employers, instead they can join a stakeholder scheme. Likewise, self-employed people can also join a stakeholder scheme.

Stakeholder schemes have a contribution limit-this being currently £3,600 per year. Anyone who is not earning can also pay into a scheme, up to the limit above. A stakeholder pension is one form of personal pension described below.

## The range of personal pensions

Personal pensions are open to anyone, in much the same way as a stakeholder scheme. These are described more fully later on in this book. Employers do not have to offer a personal pension scheme through the workplace, as they do a stakeholder scheme, though a lot do by offering a group scheme which has been separately negotiated with a provider.

## Other ways to save for retirement
### Other savings

The government offers certain tax advantages to encourage pension saving. However, the most advantageous savings plan is the Individual Savings Account (ISA) discussed further on in the book. In addition, you might have regular savings accounts, your home or a second home. All of these possibilities must be factored in when arriving at an adequate retirement income.

# 4

# Women and Pensions

It is a general rule that women pensioners tend to have less income than their male counterparts. Therefore, when building a retirement plan, women need to consider what steps they and their partners can take to make their financial future more secure.

## Particular issues for women

These days, the rules of any particular pension scheme-whether state or private, do not discriminate between men and women. Whether male or female you pay the same to access the same level of benefits. However, this does not always mean that women end up with the same level of pension as men. This is because of the general working and lifestyle differences between men and women, for example women are more likely to take breaks from work and take part time work so they can look after family. As a result, women are more likely to pay less into a pension fund than men.

Historically, the (idealised) role of women as carers was built into the UK pensions system. Not least the state pension system. It was assumed that women would marry before having children and rely on their husbands to provide for them financially right through to retirement. As a result, women who have already retired typically have much lower incomes than men.

Changes to the state scheme for people reaching state pension age from 6<sup>th</sup> April 2010 onwards, mean that most women will, in future, retire with similar state pensions as men. However if you are an unmarried women living with a partner you should be aware of the following:

- The state scheme recognises wives, husbands and civil partners but not unmarried partners. This means that if your unmarried partner dies before you, you would not be eligible for the state benefits that provide support for bereaved dependants.

- Occupational schemes and personal pensions typically pay survivor benefits to a bereaved partner, whether married or not. However many schemes-especially in the public sector-have recognised unmarried partners only recently and, as a result, the survivor pension for an unmarried partner may be very low.

- The legal system recognises that wives, husbands and civil partners may have a claim on retirement savings built up by the other party in the event of divorce, but these will be considered along with all the other assets to be split between you and you may end up with a much lower retirement income than you had been expecting.

- The legal system does not give similar rights to unmarried partners who split up. If your unmarried partner was building up pension savings for you both, he or she can walk away with all those savings and you have no legal claim on them.

# 5

## The State Pension

Over 96% of single pensioners and 99% of couples receive the basic state pension. Therefore, it is here to stay. Everyone who has paid the appropriate national insurance contributions will be entitled to a state pension. If you are not working you can either receive pension credits, as discussed, or make voluntary contributions.

The basic state pension is paid at a flat rate, currently for a single person £97.65 per week. For a couple, whether married or not, who have built up their own right to claim the basic pension could receive up to twice this amount £195.30 (2010-11). A married couple can qualify for a higher pension based on the husband's NI contributions. If the wife has reached pension age her part of the pension is paid directly to her. If the wife is below pension age, the whole pension is paid directly to the husband.

Basic state pensions are increased each April in line with price inflation. State pensioners also receive a (£10 Christmas bonus-check current entitlement) and are entitled to winter fuel payments.

At the moment, only married women can claim a pension based on their spouse's NI record. This is set to change and married men who have reached 65 will be able to claim a basic state pension based on their wife's contribution record where the wife reaches state pension age on or after 6th April 2010.

Same sex couples, as a result of the Civil Partnerships Act 2004, have the same rights as heterosexual couples in all aspects of pension provision.

## Qualifying for state pension

In order to receive the full basic pension, if you reach state pension age before 6th April 2010 the main rule is that you will have to have paid NI contributions for at least 90% of the tax years in your working life. If you have only paid for a quarter, for example, you may not get basic state pension. 'Working life' is defined as from the age 16 to retirement age, or the last complete tax year before retirement age. For men and women born after 5th March 1955 the working life is 49 years. For women with a pension age of 60, the working life is 44 years. The table overleaf indicates likely pension related to NI contributions. If you reach state pension age after 6th April 2010 then you will need 30 qualifying years in order to get the full state pension

## State pensions related to NI contributions

| Number of qualifying Years in your working Life | Fraction of the full pension | Your basic pension at 2010-2011 rates | Spouse/partner basic pension at 2010-2011 rates |
|---|---|---|---|
| 1 | 1/30 | 3.26 | 1.95 |
| 2 | 2/30 | 6.51 | 3.90 |
| 3 | 3/30 | 9.77 | 5.85 |
| 4 | 4/30 | 13.02 | 7.80 |
| 5 | 5/30 | 16.28 | 9.75 |
| 6 | 6/30 | 19.53 | 11.70 |
| 7 | 7/30 | 22.79 | 13.65 |
| 8 | 8/30 | 26.04 | 15.60 |
| 9 | 9/30 | 29.30 | 17.55 |
| 10 | 10/30 | 32.55 | 19.50 |
| 11 | 11/30 | 35.81 | 21.45 |

| 12 | 12/30 | 39.06 | 24.40 |
| --- | --- | --- | --- |
| 13 | 13/30 | 42.32 | 25.35 |
| 14 | 14/30 | 45.57 | 27.30 |
| 15 | 15/30 | 48.33 | 29.25 |
| 16 | 16/30 | 52.08 | 31.20 |
| 17 | 17/30 | 55.34 | 33.15 |
| 18 | 18/30 | 58.59 | 35.10 |
| 19 | 19/30 | 61.85 | 37.05 |
| 20 | 20/30 | 65.10 | 39.00 |
| 21 | 21/30 | 68.36 | 40.95 |
| 22 | 22/30 | 71.61 | 42.90 |
| 23 | 23/30 | 74.87 | 44.85 |
| 24 | 24/30 | 78.12 | 46.80 |
| 25 | 25/30 | 81.38 | 48.75 |
| 26 | 26/30 | 84.63 | 50.70 |
| 27 | 27/30 | 87.99 | 52.65 |
| 28 | 28/30 | 91.14 | 54.60 |
| 29 | 29/30 | 94.40 | 56.55 |
| 30 or more | 30/30 | 97.65 | 58.50 |
|  |  |  |  |

For NI contributions to count towards a state pension, they must be the right type, as the table below indicates.

## NI contributions counting towards a basic state pension.

| Type of contribution | Paid by | Details for 2010-11 |
| --- | --- | --- |
| No Contributions but earnings between LEL and PT | Employees | Earning between 97 and 110 per week |
| Class 1 full rate on earnings between PT and UAP | Employees | Earnings between 110 and 770. usually paid at 11% but less if contracted out (see further on) |
| Class 2 | Self-employed | Flat rate of 2.40 per week. Those with earnings for the year of less than 5075 can |

|  |  | choose to opt out |
| --- | --- | --- |
| Class 3 | Out of the labour market and not receiving NI credits | Flat rate of 12.05 per week |
|  |  |  |

# Key to abbreviations

LEL = Lower earnings limit: PT = Primary Threshold: UAP = Upper Accruals Point: UEL = Upper earnings limit. LEL, PT and UEL usually increase each year UAP is fixed. A rate is due to increase by 1% from 2011-2012 onwards.

**National Insurance Contributions that do not count towards the basic state pension.**

| Type of contribution | Paid By | Details for 2010-11 |
| --- | --- | --- |
| No Contributions and earnings below the LEL | Employees | Earning less than 97 |
| Class 1, married women's reduced rate | Employees | 4.85% of earnings between 110 and 844 per week and 1% above 844 (a) |
| Class 1, full rate, on earnings above the UAP | Employees | 11% of earnings between 770 and 844 per week and 1% on earnings above 844 (a) |
| No Class 2 contributions | Self-employed | Those with earnings for the year of less than 5,075 who have chosen to opt out |
| Class 4 | Self-employed | 8% of earnings for the year between 5,175 and 43,875 and 1% on earnings above 43,875 (a) |

## Class 1 contributions

Class 1 contributions are paid if earnings are above the primary threshold. The Threshold, set by government annually, is currently £110 per week (tax year 2010/11). If your earnings are above this set limit then you will be paying contributions at class 1 that build up to a state pension.

The level of contribution is set at 11% of earnings above the primary threshold level up to an upper earnings limit which is £844 per week in 2010/11. Contributions are paid at 1% of earnings above the upper earnings limit. If a person earns less than the primary threshold they will not pay NI contributions. The year will still count towards building up a basic state pension provided the earnings are not less than the lower earnings limit. This is £97 at 2010/11.

## Class 2 contributions

Self-employed people will build up their NI contributions by paying class 2 contributions. These are paid either by direct debit or by quarterly bill at the rate of £2.40 per week (2010/11).

If profits are below the 'small earnings exception' which is £5075 in 2010/11 then there is a choice of whether or not to pay NI contributions. However, if this option is chosen, then a state pension will not be building up and there could be a loss of other benefits, such as sickness, bereavement and incapacity.

If you are a director of your own company then class 1 contributions will be paid and not class 2.

## NI contribution credits

If a person is not working, in some cases they will be credited with NI contributions. This applies in the following circumstances:

- If claiming certain state benefits such as jobseekers allowance, maternity allowance or incapacity benefit
- To men and women under state pension age who have reached 60 but stopped work
- For the years in which a person has had their 16th, 17th or 18th birthday if they were still at school and were born after 5th April 1957.

If a person stays at home in order to look after children or a sick or elderly relative they might qualify for Home Responsibilities Protection. This reduces the number of years of NI contributions that are needed to qualify for a given level of pension. People who are not working and are claiming child benefit will receive Home Responsibilities Protection automatically.

## Class 3 contributions

If a person is not paying class 1 or 2 contributions or receiving HRP they can pay class 3 voluntary contributions. These are charged at a flat rate of £12.05 per week (2010/11). They can be paid up to 6 years back to make up any shortfall.

## National Insurance Credits

In some situations you may get National Insurance Credits, which plug what would otherwise be gaps in your NI record. You might get credits in the following situations.

- At the start of your working life. For the years in which you had your 16th, 17th and 18th birthdays if you were still at school and were born on or after 6th April 1957. You should get these credits automatically.

- While training. For the years in which you take part in an approved training course if you were born on or after 6th April 1957. Going to university does not count as an approved course. You should normally get these credits automatically.

- When you earn less than the lower earnings limit (£97 per week in 2010-11) and you are claiming working tax credit (or previously Working Families Tax Credit or Disabled person's Tax Credit) you should get these credits automatically.

- While temporarily working abroad if the UK has a reciprocal agreement with the country in which you are working and you are paying contributions there.

- While out of work because of unemployment or illness. If you are claiming job seekers allowance or Employment and Support Allowance, you should get these credits automatically. If you are getting Statutory Sick Pay and the year in which you get it would not otherwise be a qualifying year, you need to claim this credit by writing to the NICO Contributor Group by 31st December following the end of the tax year in which you were on sick leave.

- While you are on maternity (or adoption) leave and receiving Statutory maternity or Adoption Pay and the year in which you get it would not otherwise be a qualifying year. You need to claim this credit by writing to the NICO Contributor Group by 31$^{st}$ December following the end of the tax year in which you were on leave.

- You are a parent of a child under the age of 12 for whom you are getting child benefit. Credits are awarded automatically. You are also eligible if you are a foster carer, but in that case you will need to claim the carer's credit.

- You are a carer looking after someone with a disability or frail through old age. You get credits automatically if you are claiming Carer's Allowance. Otherwise you will need to make a claim for the Carer's Credit.

- You are on jury service and you earnings are below a certain limit (£97 a week in 2010-11). This applies to the years from 1988-89 onwards. You need to claim this credit by writing to the NICO Contributor Group by 31$^{st}$ December following the end of the tax year in which you were on jury service.

- You are a man under state pension age but older than the state pension age for women. You qualify if you are not paying NI contributions or are already getting credits for some other reason. You do not have to sign on as unemployed and should get these credits automatically.

Women's state pension age is gradually increasing and when it matches the State Pension Age for men from April 2020 onwards, this type of credit will no longer be available.

## The State Pension age

Currently, the state pension age is 65 for men. On 6$^{th}$ April 2010, the state pension age for women started to increase gradually from 60-65, to match men's. There will be further increases in the state pension age to 68 for men and women. The increase in the State Pension age is being phased in and your own particular pension age depends on when you were born. The proposed changes affect people born between April 1953 and 5$^{th}$ April 1960. The table below shows the proposed retirement ages. These changes are not yet law as they need to go to parliament for approval. (For your own retirement age you should go to the Pensions Service Website).

Table 1 indicates proposed pension changes for women.
Table 1.

| Date of Birth | Date State pension Age Reached |
|---|---|
| 6$^{th}$ April 1953 to 5$^{th}$ May 1953 | 6$^{th}$ July 2016 |
| 6$^{th}$ May 1953 to 6$^{th}$ June 1953 | 6$^{th}$ November 2016 |
| 6$^{th}$ June 1953 to 5$^{th}$ July 1953 | 6$^{th}$ March 2017 |
| 6$^{th}$ July 1953 to 5$^{th}$ August 1953 | 6$^{th}$ July 2017 |
| 6$^{th}$ August 1953 to 5$^{th}$ September 1953 | 6$^{th}$ November 2017 |
| 6$^{th}$ September 1953 to 5$^{th}$ October 1953 | 6$^{th}$ March 2018 |
| 6$^{th}$ October 1953 to 5$^{th}$ November 1953 | 6$^{th}$ July 2018 |
| 6$^{th}$ November 1953 to 5$^{th}$ December 1953 | 6$^{th}$ November 2018 |

**Table 2 overleaf.** Indicates proposed changes for men and women

35

## Table 2.

| Date of Birth | Date State Pension Age Reached |
|---|---|
| 6th December 1953 to 5th January 1954 | 6th March 2019 |
| 6th January 1954 to 5th February 1954 | 6th July 2019 |
| 6th February 1954 to 5th March 1954 | 6th November 2019 |
| 6th March 1954 to 5th April 1954 | 6th March 2010 |
| 6th April 1954 to 5th April 1960 | Your 66th Birthday |

## State pensions for people over 80

From the age of 80, all pensioners qualify for an extra 25pence per week If a person does not qualify for a basic state pension or is on a low income then they may be entitled to receive what is called ' an over-80's pension' from the age of 80.

For further advice concerning pensions either go to the government website www.thepensionsservice.gov.uk or refer to the list of useful leaflets at the back of this book.

## Additional state pension

S2P replaced the State Earnings Related Pension (SERPS) in April 2002. SERPS was, essentially, a state second tier pension and it was compulsory to pay into this in order to supplement the basic state pension. There were drawbacks however, and many people fell through the net so S2P was introduced to allow other groups to contribute. S2P refined SERPS allowing the following to contribute:

- People caring for children under six and entitled to child benefit

- Carers looking after someone who is elderly or disabled, if they are entitled to carers allowance

- Certain people who are unable to work because of illness or disability, if they are entitled to long-term incapacity benefit or severe disablement allowance and they have been in the workforce for at least one-tenth of their working life

Self-employed people are excluded from S2P as are employees earning less than the lower earnings limit. Married women and widows paying class 1 contributions at the reduced rate do not build up additional state pension. S2P is an earnings related scheme. This means that people on high earnings build up more pension than those on lower earnings. However, people earning at least the lower earnings limit (£97) in 2010/11 but less than the low earnings threshold (£110) in 2010/11 are treated as if they have earnings at that level and so build up more pension than they otherwise would.

## Contracting out

A person does not build up state additional pension during periods when they are contracted out. Contracting out means that a person has opted to join an occupational scheme or a personal pensions scheme or stakeholder pension. While contacted out, a person will pay lower National Insurance Contributions on part of earnings or some of the contributions paid by an employee and employer are 'rebated' and paid into the occupational pension scheme or other pension scheme. This is discussed more fully further on in this book.

## Increasing your state pension

There are a number of ways in which you can increase your State Pension, particularly if you have been presented with a pension forecast which shows lack of contributions and a diminished state pension. You can fill gaps in your pension contributions or you can defer your state pension. HM Revenue and Customs have a help line on 0845 915 5996 to check your record and to receive advice on whether you have gaps and how to fill them.

### Filling gaps in your record

For people reaching State Pension Age on, or after, 6$^{th}$ April 2010, you need only 30 qualifying years for the full pension. Depending on your pension age your working life may be from 44 to 52 years. Therefore, under the post April 2010 rules, you can have substantial gaps in your record without any reduction in your basic pension.

If you wish to plus gaps in your contributions, normally you can go back 6 years to fill gaps in your record. However, if you will reach State Pension Age before April 5$^{th}$ 2015, special rules let you fill any gaps up to six years in total going back as far as 6$^{th}$ April 1975. You can make class 3 contributions to fill the gap, each contribution costs £12.05 so a full years worth costs 52 times 12.05 = £626.60. Making class three contributions can't increase your additional state pension. However Class 3 contributions do count towards the state bereavement benefits that your wife, husband or civil partner could claim if you were to die.

### Deferring your state pension

Another way to boost your state pension is to delay its commencement. You can put off drawing your pension for as long as you like, there is no time limit. You must defer your whole pension, including any additional or graduated pensions and you earn an addition to the lump sum or a bigger cash sum.

In the past, if you put off drawing your own pension and your wife was getting a pension based on your NI record, her pension would also have to be deferred and she would have to agree to this. From 6th April 2010 onwards, husbands and civil partners as well as wives may be able to claim a pension based on their partners record. But a change to the rules now means that, if you defer your pension and your wife, husband or civil partner claims on your record, they no longer have to defer their pension as well.

If your pension has already started to be paid, you can decide to stop payments in order to earn extra pension or lump sum. But you can only defer your pension once. You can earn an increase in the pension when it does start of 1% for every five weeks you put off the pension. This is equivalent to an increase of 10.4% for each whole year.

Alternatively, if you put off claiming your pension for at least a whole year, you can earn a one-off lump sum instead of extra pension. The lump sum is taxable but only at the top rate you were paying before getting the lump sum. Whatever the size of the sum it does not mean that you move tax brackets.

The Pension Service publishes a detailed guide to deferring your State pension. See www.dircct.gov.uk/prod_consum_dg/groups/dg_digitalassets/@d g/@en/@over50/documents/digitalasset/dg_180189.pdf

# 6

## Changes to Private Pension Savings

In 2006, important changes were introduced to the way people save for their pensions. The cumulative changes over the years meant that the whole pension system had become very complex and some streamlining was needed.

### The lifetime allowance

From 2006, there is a single lifetime limit on the amount of savings that a person can build up through various pension schemes and plans that are subject to tax relief. (This excludes the state pension). The lifetime allowance starts at £1.8m million in the current tax year 2010/11. The LTA will be reduced to 1.5m from 6th April 2012.

The lifetime allowance applies to savings in all types of pension schemes including occupational pensions and stakeholder schemes. There are, broadly, two types of scheme or plan:

- Defined contribution-with these types of schemes money goes in and is invested with the fund used to buy a pension. Basically, if the fund at retirement is £200,000 then £200,000 lifetime allowance has been used up

- Defined benefit-in this type of scheme, a person is promised a pension of a certain amount usually worked out on the basis of salary before retirement and the length of time that you have been in the scheme. The equation for working out lifetime benefit in this type of scheme is a little more complicated. The pension is first converted into a notional sum (the amount of money it is reckoned is needed to buy a pension of that size). The government sets out a factor that it says will be needed to make the conversion which it has said is 20. If the pension is £20,000 then this is calculated as £20,000 times £20,000 which is £400,000. Therefore £400,000 will be used up from the lifetime allowance.

## The annual allowance

In addition to the lifetime allowance, there will be a lifetime allowance starting at £255,000 in 2010/11. This will fall to 50,000 for 2011/12. This is the amount that pension savings may increase each year whether through contributions paid in or to promised benefits. An addition to the promised benefits must be converted to a notional lump sum before it can be compared with the annual allowance. The government has stated that a factor of 10 should be used as a multiplier. For example, if a promised pension increases by £300, this is equivalent to a lump sum of 10 times £300 = £3,000, therefore using up £3000 of the annual allowance. The limit will be revised each year and can be obtained from the government pensions website www.thepensionsservice.gov.uk.

The annual allowance will not start in the year a person starts their pension or die. This gives a person scope to make large last-minute additions to their fund.

If at retirement the value of a pension exceeds the lifetime allowance there will be an income tax charge of 55% on the excess if it is taken as a lump sum, or 25% if it is left in the scheme to be taken as a pension, which is taxable as income.

If the increase in the value of savings in any year exceeds the annual allowance, the excess is taxed at 40%.

## Limits to benefits and contributions

The present benefit and contribution limits have been scrapped. The only remaining restrictions are:

- Contributions-the maximum that can be paid in each year is either the amount equal to taxable earnings or £3,600 whichever is the greater

- Tax free lump sum-at retirement a person can take up to one quarter of the value of the total pension fund as a tax free lump sum

In the case of death before retirement, in general savings can be paid out to survivors either as an income or as a lump sum. A lump sum up to the value of the lifetime limit will be tax-free but anything over will be taxed at 55%.

If a person leaves a scheme before two years membership they can take a refund of contributions. Refunds are paid after deduction of tax at 20% on the first £10,800 and 40% on any excess.

Tax relief on contributions will either be given at source or through PAYE if relevant.

## Starting a pension

With the exception of ill-health, a person must start their pension at a minimum age, currently 50 but due to rise to 55 by 2010 and maximum age 75. Schemes will administer the rules for retirement in the minimum age to 55. Special rules will safeguard the rights of people in certain occupations to retire earlier provided they had this right already on 10th December 2003, but the lifetime limit will be reduced where it is to be applied at an earlier age. The reduction will be 2.5% of the limit for every year in advance of age 55. Any unused part of the lifetime allowance can be carried forward to set against future pension earnings.

## Taking a pension

Savings do not have to be converted into pension in one go. This can be staggered and pension income can be increased as a person winds down from work.

For each tranche of pension started before 75, there is a range of choices. This will depend on the rules of each individual scheme. A person can:

- Have a pension paid direct from an occupational pension scheme

- Use a pension fund to purchase an annuity to provide a pension for the rest of life

- Use part of the pension to buy a limited period annuity lasting just five years leaving the rest invested

- Opt for income drawdown which allows taking of a pension whilst leaving the rest invested. The tax-free lump sum could be taken and the rest left invested. The maximum income will be 120% of a standard annuity rate published by the Financial Services Authority. On death the remaining pension fund can be used to provide pensions for dependants or paid to survivors as a lump sum, taxed at 35%.

When a person reaches 75 years of age, they must opt for one of the following choices:

- Have a pension paid direct from an occupational scheme

- Use the pension fund to buy an annuity to provide a pension for the rest of life or

- Opt for an Alternatively Secured Pension or ASP. This is pension draw down but with the maximum income limited to 70% of the annuity rate for a 75 year old, the minimum income is nil. On death, the remaining fund can be used to provide dependants pensions or, if there are no dependants, left to a charity or absorbed into the scheme to help other people's pensions. The person(s) whose pensions are to be enhanced can be nominated by the person whose pension it is.

# 7

## Job Related Pensions

The best way to save for retirement is through an occupational pension scheme. Employers will also contribute and pay administration costs. Schemes normally provide an additional package of benefits such as protection if you become disabled, protection for dependants and protection against inflation. Some pension schemes are related to final salary and provide a pension that equates to a proportion of salary. However, it must be said that a lot of these schemes are winding down.

### Limits on your pension savings
These limits apply collectively to all private pensions (occupational schemes and personal pensions) that you may have)

| Type of limit | Description | Amount |
|---|---|---|
| Annual contribution limit | The maximum contributions on which you can get tax relief. You can continue contributing to your 75th birthday | £3,600 or 100% of your UK relevant earnings for the year whichever is the greater |
| Annual allowance | The maximum addition to your pension savings in any one year (including for example employers contributions). Anything above the limit normally triggers a tax charge, but this does not apply in the year that you start to draw the pension. | Tax year 2010/11 £255,000 but falling to 50,000 tax year 2011/12 |

| Lifetime allowance | The cumulative value of benefits that can be drawn from your pension savings. Any amount drawn that exceeds the limits triggers a tax charge. | Tax year 2010/11<br><br>£1.8 Million falling to 1.5m from 6th April 2012. |
|---|---|---|

## Tax advantages of occupational schemes

The tax advantages of occupational schemes are:

- A person receives tax relief on the amount that he or she pays into the scheme

- Employers contributions count as a tax-free benefit

- Capital gains on the contributions build up tax free

- At retirement part of the pension fund can be taken as a tax-free lump sum. The rest is taken as a taxable pension

People aged 65 and over receive more generous tax allowances than younger people. Tax allowances are dealt with further on in the book.

### Qualifying to join an occupational scheme

An occupational scheme can be either open to all or restricted to certain groups, i.e. different schemes for different groups. Schemes are not allowed to discriminate in terms of race or gender or any other criteria. Employees do not have to join a scheme and can leave when they wish. There might however be restrictions on rejoining or joining a scheme later on.

Not all employers offer an occupational scheme. Another pension arrangement such as a stakeholder scheme or Group Pension Scheme might be offered.

The amount of pension that a person receives from an occupational scheme will depend in part on the type of scheme that it is. Currently, there are two main types:

- Defined benefit schemes, promising a given level of benefit on retirement, usually final salary schemes

- Money purchase schemes (defined contribution schemes), where a person builds up their own savings pot. There are hybrid schemes where both the above are on offer but these are not common.

### Final salary schemes
With final salary schemes, a person is promised (but not guaranteed) a certain level of pension and other benefits related to earnings. This is independent of what is paid into the scheme. Final salary schemes work well when a person stays with their employer for a long length of time or work in the public sector.

A person in such a scheme will typically pay around 5% of their salary into the scheme with the employer paying the balance of the cost which will be around 10% of salary on average. When the stock market is doing well the employer is safeguarded but when the economic climate is changing, such as at this point in time then the story is somewhat different and the employer has to pay more to maintain the level of pension. This is why such pension schemes are being withdrawn.

The pension received at retirement is based on a formula and related to final salary and years of membership in the scheme. The maximum usually builds up over 40 years. The accrual rate in such a scheme is one sixtieth or one eightieth of salary per year in the scheme.

If a person leaves the pension scheme before retirement they are still entitled to receive a pension from the scheme, based on contributions.

### 'Final salary' defined

The final salary is defined in the rules of the scheme. It can have a variety of meanings, for example average pay over a number of years, average of the best salary for a number of years out of ten, or earnings on a specified date. What counts are the pensionable earnings, which may mean basic salary, or could include other elements such as overtime, bonus etc.

A lump sum tax-free is included in the scheme which is defined by HMRC rules. The lump sum after 40 years of service will be around 1.5 times the annual salary.

### Money purchase schemes

Money purchase pension schemes are like any other forms of savings or investment. Money is paid in and grows in value and the proceeds eventually provide a pension. The scheme is straightforward and has its upsides and downsides. The upside is that it is simple and portable. The downside is that it is related to the growth of the economy and can shrink as well as grow.

It is more difficult to plan for retirement with this kind of scheme, as distinct from the final salary scheme. As we have seen, employers prefer this kind of scheme because, although they pay into it, it doesn't place any onerous responsibilities on them.

The pension that is received on retirement will depend on the amount paid into the scheme, charges deducted for management of the scheme, how well the investment grows and the rate, called the annuity rate, at which the fund can be converted into pension. A major problem for pension schemes has been the decline in annuity rates in recent years.

With most money purchase schemes the proceeds are usually given to an insurer who will administer the funds. The trustees of the scheme will choose the insurer, in most cases. In some cases, contributors are given the choice of investment. This choice will usually include:

- A with-profits basis which is a medium-risk option and which is safer and more likely to provide a good return if a person remains with the same employer. The value of the fund cannot fall and will grow steadily as reversionary bonuses are added. On retirement a person will receive a terminal bonus, which represents a chunk of the overall return

- A unit linked fund- where money is invested in one or more funds, e.g. shares, property, gilts and so on.

### The cash balance scheme
A cash balance scheme lies somewhere between a final salary scheme and a money purchase scheme. Whereas in a final salary scheme a person is promised a certain level of pension at retirement with a cash balance scheme a person is promised a

certain amount of money with which to buy a pension. The amount of cash can be expressed in a number of ways, for example as a percentage of salary per annum for each year of membership. So if a person is earning £50,000 per annum and the cash balance scheme is promising 15% of salary for each year of membership, there would be a pension fund of £50,000 times 15% which equals £75,000 after 10 years of membership.

## Tax

Whichever type of pension that is offered, the government sets limits on maximum amounts that a person can receive. HMRC sets limits on occupational schemes which relate mainly to final salary schemes and which are shown below.

## Main HMRC limits on pensions.

1.  If you are in a scheme set up on or after 14th March 1989 or a scheme set up before 14th March 1989 but you joined on or after 1st June 1989, or are in a scheme set up before 14th March 1989 which you joined on or after 17th March 1987 but before 1st June 1989 if you elected to be treated under the 'post 1989 regime'.

Under the above rules you will get a percentage of final salary up to £68,000 with a limit on the lump sum at retirement of 1.5 times final salary up to a maximum of £150,000. These are the limits for the current tax year.

2.  If you are in a scheme set up before 14th March 1989 which was joined on or after 17th March 1987 and before 1st June 1989 you will receive a percentage of final salary up to a maximum of 1.5 times salary or £150,000.

If you joined a scheme before 17<sup>th</sup> March 1987 you will receive a percentage of final salary up to 1.5 times salary.

Normally, the maximum pension and any other benefits build up over a long period, usually 40 years. The pension builds up at a rate of one sixtieth of final salary for each year that you are with the employer. The maximum lump sum builds up at a rate of three-eightieths of final salary.

The rules allow for a faster build up of pension if a person can't build up pension over such a long period.

The pension scheme will set a pension age, and although there used to be difference in the age at which pension was paid to men and women respectively, the dates are now usually harmonised. The most popular age for receiving pension is 65 although some opt for 60. The lowest age at which pensions can be paid is 50. In most cases, a person must give up a job before receiving an occupational pension from an employer. The rules are in the process of changing so that a pension can be received from an employer whilst still working for that employer.

Tax rules set a limit on the amount that a pension can be increased each year. This is usually inflation. If the starting pension is less than the Inland Revenue maximum then bigger increases are allowed. For pensions built up from April 6<sup>th</sup> 1997 onwards the increase is limited to a limited price indexation which means that each year the pension can be increased in line with inflation up to a maximum of 2.5% per year.

### Contributions into occupational schemes

Some occupational schemes are non-contributory, which means that the employer pays all contributions. The majority of schemes, however, are contributory, with the employer and employee contributing. Usually, the employee will pay 5% of salary. With money purchase schemes the employer will also pay a specified amount of salary. With final salary schemes, which as stated are becoming less and less common, the employer will make up the balance needed to provide the specified amount.

Both employer and employee will get tax relief on contributions.

Top-up schemes exist which can be used to top up pension pots but these are liable for tax in the usual way. There are two main types of top-up scheme:

- Unfunded schemes. With these schemes, an employer simply pays benefits at the time that a person reaches retirement. Income tax will be due on any benefits, even on lump sums

- funded schemes (Funded Unapproved Retirement Benefit Schemes or FURBS). This is where the employer pays contributions which build up funds to provide the eventual benefits. At the time that contributions are made they count as tax-liable fringe benefits. Usually the fund is arranged as a trust, which attracts only normal rates of tax. The benefits are tax-free when they are paid out, having been subject to tax.

If an employer runs a scheme which a person is eligible to join they must be given information about it automatically. The rules are as follows:

- an explanatory booklet must be given within two months of commencing employment if eligible to join, or within 13 weeks of joining

- each year a summary trustees report an annual accounts must be given

- employees can request a copy of the full accounts which must be provided on request

- an annual benefit statement must be provided

- options on leaving the scheme and benefit entitlements, transfer value must be provided within 3 months of request

- any announcements of changes to the scheme must be given to the scheme member within one month of the change being made

Information about employer schemes can be found in various booklets listed in the appendix to this book.

# 8

## Group Personal Pension Schemes

Group personal pension schemes are a popular alternative to occupational pension schemes, particularly to smaller employers.

Group personal pension schemes are not occupational pension schemes. They are pension schemes tailored to employees of a company. The employer is not obliged to pay anything into such schemes, although many do. The amount an employer will pay is often less than an occupational pension scheme. The employee will usually end up contributing more.

Group personal pension schemes work on a money purchase basis, and, as we have seen, the employee will bear all the risks themselves. The administration charges for group personal pension schemes are usually the same as other pension funds. A plus side of group schemes is that they are seen to be particularly suitable for employees on short term contracts who cannot build up reasonable benefits in an occupational scheme because of frequent job changes. Group pension schemes are personal and travel with the employee and can be kept going without a break.

### Group Personal pension Schemes and stakeholder schemes

Since October 2001, employers with more than five employees must offer at least an occupational pension scheme, a group scheme or a stakeholder scheme to employees. Stakeholder schemes are outlined further on in the book.

The pension on retirement from a group scheme will depend on the same factors as all money purchase schemes, such as the overall amount paid in and the performance of the investment. In addition, the charges taken to administer the scheme will influence the amount left in the pot.

In terms of receipt of a tax-free lump sum, group schemes are exactly the same as all other pension funds.

************

# 9

## Contracting Out Through Occupational Schemes

---

Employees who are building up a state additional pension can contract out, which means that a person gives up their additional state pension and instead builds up a replacement through an occupational scheme or a personal pension scheme.

Contracting out essentially means that a person receives less pension at retirement from the state. Because this saves the state money then it pays back part of the NI contributions that the employee and employer are paying now. These repayments are invested in the personal or occupational scheme to raise its value. Contracting out has not benefited everyone and how much it benefits an individual depends on how much is given up on the value of the additional state pension. This in turn depends very much on the type of scheme that is used to contract out. Although in many cases, an individual has the choice whether or not to contract out, if an employee belongs to a contracted out fund then the choice has already been made. The only way to rejoin S2P would be to leave the scheme.

### How contracting out operates in an occupational scheme
As stated, if a person is contracted out in an occupational pension scheme, then both employee and employer will pay lower NI contributions which are reinvested in the scheme.

### Contracting out before 6th April 1997
During the period between 6th April 1978 and 6th April 1997, contracting out meant giving up the State Earnings Related

Pension (SERPS). For pension rights built up over the period up to 6<sup>th</sup> April 1997, the occupational scheme guarantees to pay a minimum amount of pension at retirement, known as a Guaranteed Minimum Pension (GMP). It will also pay a guaranteed widow's or widowers pension. This Guaranteed Pension will be broadly equivalent to the amount that would have been built up in SERPS.

Contracted out final salary pension rights are different for pensions built up from 6<sup>th</sup> April 1997. A person no longer builds up any Guaranteed Pension Rights. Instead the employer must run a scheme which, for nine out of ten scheme members, is at least as good as a reference scheme which has been specified by the government. The main elements of such a reference scheme are that it must provide:

- a retirement pension at age 65 equal to one eightieth of qualifying earnings for each year of membership since April 1997, up to a maximum pension of half average earnings. Earnings to be used in the calculation are 90% of total earnings, including overtime and bonuses etc, above the lower earnings limit up to the upper limit. Earnings for the last three years before retirement or leaving the scheme are averaged. The pension must be the same for both men and women and can be paid before 65 but will be reduced.
- A widows or widowers pension equal to half the retirement pension built up if the scheme member dies either while working, after retirement or having moved on to another job while leaving the pension behind in the previous employers scheme

- Annual increases to pensions, once they start to be paid, of inflation up to 5% maximum.

Each scheme has to have a certificate from an actuary stating that its benefits are sufficient to pass the contracting out test.

## Rules for contracting out from 6th April 2002

From 6th April 2002, a person contracts out of S2P instead of SERPS. As discussed, pensions provided by S2P for people on low to moderate incomes are higher than SERPS. To ensure that people still had an incentive to contract out of S2P certain rules were introduced. People earning less than the Band 3 threshold will continue to build up some residual S2P pension even though are contracted out. This means that at retirement they will get some enhanced pension through S2P.

For people earning between the lower earnings limit and the low earning threshold, their residual SERPS pension will be based on the difference between their actual earnings and the low earnings threshold. For people earning more than the low earnings threshold up to the Band 3 threshold their residual S2P will be based on the difference between the SERPS pension they would have had if SERPS had not been abolished and the S2P they would have had if they had not contracted out. There are no special rules for people above the Band 3 threshold, because for them S2P is the same as SERPS pension they would have got had SERPS not been abolished.

## Contracting out through an occupational money purchase scheme00

Contracting out through an occupational money purchase scheme is different. Employer and employee still both pay lower

NI contributions. However, the employer scheme makes no guarantee about how much it will pay to replace the state pension. Instead the employer is required to guarantee that they will pay a set amount into the scheme that will build up the fund. The amounts invested are equal to the amounts that the employer and the employee have saved by paying lower NI contributions. The fund that is built up provides a set of benefits called 'protected rights' which comprise:

- a retirement pension which can be paid from age 60 onwards

- a pension for widow or widower if a person dies before retirement

- a pension for widow or widower if death happens if death occurs after retirement which is equal to half the pension that is received. A person can opt for a larger pension for their self with no provision for widow or widower

- increases to pensions once they start to be paid. Although this requirement may be removed.

After April 2006 up to a quarter of the pension savings can be taken as a tax-free lump sum.

Protected rights benefits build up on a money purchase basis so the amount of money that you receive as a pension will depend on:

- The amount invested

- Charges deducted from the scheme

- How well the investment does

- The rate (annuity rate) at which the pension fund can be converted into a pension.

## Contracting out before 6<sup>th</sup> April 1997 and after 6<sup>th</sup> April 1997

Up to 6<sup>th</sup> April 1997 the amount of National Insurance rebate which an employer was obliged to invest for protected rights was a flat rate, the same for everyone. Where a person has built up protected rights before 6<sup>th</sup> April 1997, the DWP will work out the full SERPS pension that a person would have built up had they not contracted out. The amount built up is called the 'notional GMP' and it may be more or less than the protected rights pension that is received from the contracted out scheme. Whatever is left after subtracting the notional GMP is the amount of SERPS pension that will be received from the state.

From 1997 onwards, the rules for rebates changed. They are now age related. The older a person is the larger the rebate.

## Personal pension plans

If an employer's pension scheme is not contracted out of the state scheme a person can opt to contract out on his or her own through a special personal pension called a 'rebate-only' plan. If a person belongs to a group personal pension scheme offered by an employer they will have their own personal pension plan.

## Free-standing Additional Voluntary Contributions

If a person belongs to an employer scheme that is not contracted out they can contract out independently using a free-standing additional voluntary contribution scheme instead of a personal pension. However, it is usually better to take out a personal pension plan as overall the benefits are better. The DWP pays less into a contracted out AVC scheme than it does into a contracted out personal pension.

## Other benefits from occupational schemes

Occupational pensions schemes, as opposed to group personal or stakeholder pension schemes, automatically provide packages of benefits. These will include:

- Lump-sum life cover and dependants pensions if death occurs before retirement

- Dependants pensions if death occurs after retirement

- Replacement income if a person has to give up work early because of ill-health or disability

- A pension if retirement occurs before normal retirement age

HM Revenue and Customs sets limits on the amounts that dependants can receive by way of pension after death.

Like the retirement pension itself, the benefits are subsidised because the employer pays some or all of the costs of provision, and a person will get tax relief on the contributions.

A widow's or widower's pension is usually paid automatically to wife or husband. partner or civil partner. Most occupational schemes usually allow the pension to be paid to someone else at the trustee's discretion. If the trustee's decide that there is no eligible person to receive it then the money remains in the scheme.

Pensions can be paid to other dependants, such as children in addition to any amount paid to a widow, widower or partner. Any one pension cannot be more than two-thirds of the maximum retirement pension that the person would have received if he or she had been alive. A pension for a dependant child ceases when that child ceases to be dependant, for example when the child reaches the age of 18, or when he or she finishes full-time education. Pensions for other dependants can continue for the rest of their lives even if they cease to be dependant.

### Early retirement due to ill-health

There are no HMRC limits on the age that a person can receive a pension if they have to retire through ill-health. A person does not have to be completely incapable of work to qualify for the pension. If health is sufficiently bad to prevent a person from pursuing a normal course of work then this will qualify. However, evidence of ill-health will be needed and each scheme will set its own rules. Tax limits on the pension that is received are more generous than those that apply to retirement for other reasons. The pensions and benefits that are received cannot be more than the pension that would be received had a person worked until normal retirement age.

If a person is severely ill and not expected to live long then the pension can be converted into a lump sum. There is a tax charge of 20% on the part that could not be taken as a tax-free lump sum.

### Early retirement generally

For pension schemes set up before 14th March 1989, tax rules will normally prohibit an employer pension scheme from paying a full pension before the normal retirement age for the scheme. For these schemes, the earliest retirement age allowed by HMRC is either 55 or 60, depending on when the scheme was set up and when it was joined. In practice, most schemes set their own early retirement age later than this. The most common retirement age is 65, the second most common is 60.

From 6th April 2010 the earliest retirement age is 55.

# 10

## Leaving an Occupational Scheme

There are a number of reasons why people may want to leave an occupational scheme before retirement. One of the main ones is leaving an employer to take up another job. It could be that there is a desire to leave one pension scheme and enter another. Whatever the reason, there are a number of questions that need answering.

If a person leaves an occupational pension fund and has been a member of it for two years or more that scheme must provide a pension at retirement, called a deferred pension, or allow transfer of the contributions. A new pension scheme is not legally obliged to accept transfer.

### Obtaining a refund of contributions

If a person leaves a scheme that he or she has belonged to for less than two years, there is no automatic entitlement to a refund or pension. A person can have back any contributions that they themselves paid but not their employer. Tax is paid on any refund. There may also be a deduction. A significant reduction, if a person had been contracted out of SERPS prior to April 1997 through the occupational scheme. The scheme may arrange for a person to be 'bought back into' the state scheme for the period that has been contracted out. This will cost a sum of money, called the Contribution Equivalent Premium, to the state.

For periods of contracting out after April 1997, it is no longer possible for a person to be bought back into SERPS, if membership of the scheme has been less than two years.

If a person has contracted out through a final-salary scheme and leaves, the scheme is obliged to protect contracted out pension rights. For contracted out pension rights built up before April 1997, a person is entitled to a Preserved Guaranteed Minimum Pension (GMP) and widow's or widower's pension. The amount of GMP is calculated and increased from the date that a person leaves a pension. The increase can either be in line with inflation, in line with average earnings, or by a fixed amount. GMP's can be transferred to another scheme or plan as long as that scheme or plan can be used for contracted out pension rights.

For periods of contracting out after 6th April 1997, a person can no longer build up GMPs. Instead the scheme has to provide a person with a scheme of benefits that is at least as good as those from a reference scheme. If a person leaves the scheme and leaves the benefits there then they must be increased by inflation up to a maximum each year. If a person leaves a contracted out money purchase scheme that scheme must continue to provide protected rights. Stories of people losing touch with their pensions over the years are legion and it is very important to stay in touch with the scheme and inform them of change of address and change of circumstances. There is the right to request a statement of benefits once every twelve months.

# 11

## Transferring Pension Rights

Since 1$^{st}$ January 1986 anyone leaving an employer pension scheme who has a right to a preserved pension also has the right to take a transfer value instead. This is a lump sum that is judged to be equivalent to the preserved pension and any other rights given up. This cannot be received in the hand but can be transferred.

If pension rights are switched from an occupational money purchase scheme, the transfer value will quite simply be the value of that fund. If the switch is from a final salary scheme the transfer value must be worked out by an actuary. Assumptions are made about future investment growth and a lump sum to be transferred is arrived at.

If a person transfers into a money purchase scheme the sum is simply added to the fund. If it is transferred into a final salary scheme the transfer might be used to buy a fixed amount of pension at retirement, buy extra years in a fund or invested as a separate fund to be used at retirement to buy 'extra benefits' in a scheme. The pension fund that is the recipient of the fund will provide advice in this area.

### Transfer to a Section 32 plan

Section 32 plans – termed buy-back bonds – are a special type of personal pension designed to accept transfer value from occupational pension schemes. The transfer value is simply transferred into the plan and used to buy a deferred annuity, which is an insurance product designed to pay out an income starting at a future date.

The decision whether to transfer from a previous employers occupational scheme has never been an easy one and many people feel that they will suffer a shortfall if they do. The benefits of transfer need to be weighed up on the basis of what information can be gathered from the new provider.

Public sector transfers can be easier as 'transfer clubs' exist. This is related to final salary schemes and allows the transfer years that have been built up to be added to the new schemes.

It is the transfer from an employer's occupational scheme to a personal pension scheme that can be problematic and where losses can occur. If the old scheme is a final salary scheme there will inevitably be loss of benefits associated with the old scheme, benefits such as transferring pension to dependants if death occurs. With occupational schemes quite often the employer will bear the cost of administration expenses whereas this will not be the case with a personal pension scheme.

Therefore, a lot of thought needs to be given to transferring into a personal pensions scheme, and as much information as possible gathered before doing so.

## Winding up of occupational pension schemes
If an occupational scheme is wound up by an employer, for whatever reason, for example bankruptcy or being taken over by another firm which doesn't wish to continue the scheme, the pension entitlement from the scheme will depend on the rules of

the particular scheme. Whilst some are generous others may provide only the minimum entitlement.

There are rules which make any shortfall in final salary schemes a debt of the company. Where bankruptcy occurs the debt will rank alongside that of other unsecured creditors. This is not a good position to be in as it invariably means that pensions become non-existent, although since September 2003, the position of unsecured creditors in relation to pension rights became a little stronger. There is a pecking order, as there always is in bankruptcy and the rights of those with pension funds can be obtained from the government insolvency service website. See also useful addresses at the back of this book.

# 12

## New Duties for Employers Relating to Provision of Pensions from 2012

From 2012, changes to pensions law will affect all employers with at least one worker in the UK.

Employers will need to:

- Automatically enrol certain workers into a pension scheme

- Make contributions on their workers behalf

- Register with the Pensions Regulator

- Provide workers with information about the changes and how they will affect them.

The new employer duties will be introduced in stages over 4 years, starting in 2012. Each employer will be allocated a date from when the duties will first apply to them, know as their 'staging date'. This date is based on the number of people in an employer's PAYE scheme. Employers with the largest number of employee's in their PAYE scheme will have the earliest staging date.

These staging dates can be checked on www.tpr.gov.uk/staging.

## Automatic enrolment

Workers who need to be automatically enrolled are called' eligible jobholders'. An eligible jobholder is:

- Aged between 22 and the state pension age

- Working, or ordinarily working in the UK

- Earning above a certain amount (currently proposed to be £7,475).

The location of the employer is not relevant when considering if the worker is an eligible jobholder. Neither is the worker's nationality or the length of their stay in the UK.

When considering whether a workers earnings are above or below the lower earnings limit, an employer needs to look at what is known as the workers 'qualifying earnings'. This will include earnings in salary, overtime, commission, bonuses, sick pay, maternity, paternity and adoption pay.

## Choosing a pension scheme

Employers with an automatic enrolment duty will need to choose a pension scheme they can use for automatic enrolment. Information from the Pensions Regulator will be available to help inform this decision.

Employers might use an existing scheme or set up a new one with a pension provider.

In addition, there is the National Employment Savings Trust (NEST). NEST is a pension scheme with the following characteristics:

- It has a public service obligation, meaning it must accept all employers who apply.

- It has been established by government to ensure that employers, including those that employ low to medium earners, can access pension savings and comply with their automatic enrolment duties.

Whether the scheme an employer uses for automatic enrolment is new or not, it must meet certain specific set out in legislation.

The scheme cannot:

- Impose barriers, such as probationary periods or age limits for workers.

- Require staff to make an active choice to join or take other action, e.g. having to sign a form or provide extra information to the scheme themselves, either prior to joining or to retain active membership of the scheme.

Each pension scheme will have its own rules, but all employers will need to provide the scheme with certain information about the person who is automatically enrolled.

### Employers/employee contributions

Many employers offer a defined contribution scheme to staff. The rules of these schemes must require the employer to pay an overall minimum contribution of at least 8% of the workers qualifying earnings, of which at least 3% must be from the employer.

In most cases, government tax relief will account for 1% of the total 8%.

Employers who already have a pension scheme can confirm that it is suitable for automatic enrolment by a process called 'certification'.

## Opt-out

Workers who have been automatically enrolled have the right to opt out of the employer's pension scheme by effectively giving one months notice. To opt out, workers must give notice via an 'opt out' notice to the employer. When employers receive a valid opt out notice within the 1-month period, they must pay back any contributions deducted from the workers pay.

## Other workers

As well as automatically enrolling eligible jobholders, employers must also put certain other workers into a pension scheme, if these individuals ask. More information will be available from the Pensions Regulator later this year. Their website is www.thepensionsregulator.gov.uk.

# 13

## Pensions and Benefits for Dependants

### State pensions

If you die before your spouse or civil partner has reached state pension age there may be some entitlement to state bereavement benefits if you have built up the appropriate NI contributions in the years prior to your death.

The following may be available:

- Bereavement payment. This is a tax-free lump sum of £2000

- Widowed Parent's Allowance. This is a taxable income set at the same level as the basic state pension (£97.65 per week 2010-2011) plus half of any additional state pension (S2P) you had built up. The payment continues until the youngest child ceases to be dependant or until your widow, widower or civil partner, enters a new marriage or civil partnership or starts to live with someone as if they were married or registered. Your spouse or civil partner might also be able to claim Child tax credit (CTC, a means tested state benefit available to households with children).

- Bereavement allowance. This is a regular taxable payment payable to spouses and civil partners over age 45 without any dependant children. The amount increases with their age. This is payable for a maximum of 52 weeks and will cease if a spouse or civil partner remarries.

### Death after retirement

If you die after you and your spouse/civil partner have both reached State Pension age

Help is given through the State pension system. Your spouse or partner, if they do not receive a full basic pension in their own right, may be able to make up the pension to the full single person's rate (£97.65 per week 2010-11) by using your contribution record. In addition, they can inherit half of any additional State Pension you had built up.

To find out more about bereavement benefits contact your local jobcentre plus, if you are of working age at www.direct.gov.uk. Advice on a full range of bereavement benefits for those who are retired can also be obtained here.

### Occupational and personal schemes

Occupational and personal schemes may also offer pensions and lump sum pay-outs for your survivors when you die.

Schemes can pay pensions to your dependants (but not anyone who was not dependant or co-dependant on you) whether you die before or after you started your pension. This means your husband, wife, civil partner, children under the age of 23 or, if older, dependant on you because of physical or mental impairment. Also, anyone else financially dependant on you can benefit.

Under the tax rules, all the dependants pensions added together must not come to more than the retirement pension you would have been entitled to, but otherwise there is no limit on the amount of any one pension, although individual scheme rules may set some limits.

## Dependant's pensions from occupational salary-related schemes

Subject to tax rules governing such schemes, a scheme can set its own rules about how much pension it will provide for dependants. Typically, a scheme will provide a pension for a widow, widower, civil partner or unmarried partner on:

* death before you have started your pension

* death after you have started your pension.

* This will typically be half or two thirds of the pension that you were entitled to at the time of your death. The pension must be increased in line with inflation. If you have been contracted out through a salary related pension scheme before April 1977, the scheme must pay a guaranteed minimum pension (GMP) to the person entitled equal to half the GMP's you had built up.

## Lump sum death benefits

The types of lump sum that can be paid out and how they are treated for tax depends on your pension arrangement and your age at the time of death. Although the key age at which the rules change has been 75 years, this is to be relaxed and consultation is taking place. At the moment the age has now been increased to 77 and is likely to increase further following consultation.

If you die before 75, and before starting your pension, an occupational scheme or personal pension may pay out a lump sum, tax-free. This can be paid to anyone-they do not have to be your dependant. The amount paid out is tested against your lifetime allowance, as described earlier. If it comes to more than your remaining allowance, the excess sum is taxed at 55%.

If you die before 75 but have already started your pension, or an income withdrawal arrangement, or if you have reached 75 on, or after, 22nd June 2010 and you have not started your pension, the following lump sums might be available but taxed at 35%:

- Pension or annuity with a guarantee period-typically the period is five or ten years

- Annuity protection-an annuity may guarantee to pay out at least as much as its purchase price

- Income withdrawal-if you had opted for income withdrawal, the remainder of the pension fund that has not been paid out in pension can be paid on death as a lump-sum.

# 14

## Protecting Pensions

It is not surprising that people get very disillusioned and nervous when it comes to pensions. Since the 1980's there have been a number of scandals involving blatant theft of pensions (Robert Maxwell), and also incidences of mis-selling.

During the 1950's, one of Britain's biggest insurance companies, Equitable life, offered pensions which were supposed to guarantee a fixed level of income at retirement. However, by the 1990's these guarantees became too expensive and the company could not fulfill their promises. Equitable life faced many legal challenges and stopped taking on any new business. Many pensioners found themselves with poor returns and it is only now that the government is looking at compensating the victims.

In addition to theft and bad management the usual raft of 'financial advisors' mis-sold personal pensions, taking advantage particularly of the changes in the 1980's and people confusion. Although many people received compensation, many others did not and a lot of distress was caused to a lot of people.

To add to the above a lot of companies became insolvent and there was too little in the pension funds to fulfill pension promises. In the early days (early 2000's) there was a spate of these insolvencies and lots of people lost their pension or received less than they had planned for. The government set up several schemes to help such people and a compensation scheme was set up to assist.

The main risk to pension funds lies with occupational schemes. Although people need to be aware of changes to the state pension scheme it is safe in so far as the state is unlikely to become insolvent and unable to pay. For sure people need to keep abreast of legislation and changes to state pensions but in essence the amount promised will remain safe.

## Occupational schemes

As discussed above, one of the main risks to occupational pensions is that the employer might embezzle the funds. This should be difficult given the role of the pension trustees, which will be outlined below, but it is always possible. There is also the risk that the scheme cannot pay the amount promised. This can be to do with stock market fluctuations, or, as we have all painfully seen in the last few years, a deep recession which affects people and pensions globally.

Another problem that may arise is that of schemes with defined benefits, final salary schemes, changing their rules and replacing defined benefits with less generous schemes.

## Protecting pensions

Occupational schemes are usually either statutory schemes or are set up under a trust. A statutory scheme is as the name implies. It is set up under an Act of Parliament and is the usual arrangement for most public sector schemes such as police, NHS, teachers and so on. Private sector schemes are usually always set up under a trust. This ensures that the scheme is kept at arms length from the employer and business, and can't go down with the sinking ship. (Many lessons have been learned post-Robert Maxwell). With a trust you will have three main elements:

- The sponsor, who will be the employer, who will initially decide on the rules of the scheme along with the benefits

- the beneficiaries, who are scheme members and any beneficiaries who might benefit if, say, a scheme member passes away

- Very importantly, the trustees who are tasked with looking after the pension fund and making sure that it is administered in accordance with the scheme rules.

The trustees are responsible for the running of the scheme but can also employ outside help, specialist help and can employ someone to administrate the scheme. They are supported in this role by the Pensions Regulator, which is the official body that regulates all worked based schemes (occupational schemes and also those personal pensions and stakeholder schemes organized through the workplace). The Pensions Regulator promotes good practice, monitors risk, investigates schemes and responds to complaints from scheme members. The Pensions Regulator has many powers, as would be expected, and can prosecute those who it thinks guilty of wrongdoing.

There is a Fraud Compensation Fund which can pay out where an occupational pension schemes assets have been embezzled or reduced because of dishonest activity. The fund is financed by a levy on all occupational pension schemes.

### Other schemes

Normally, if there is a shortfall when a pension scheme is wound up, the employer would be expected to make up any shortfall. However, clearly this is not possible if the employer is insolvent and there is no money to put into a scheme. Between 1997 and 2005 some 85,000 people lost some or all of their promised pensions because of insolvency. Because of this several schemes were set up to provide protection:

- Financial Assistance Scheme (FAS). This scheme was set up and funded by the government to provide help for those pensions scheme members in greatest need where their pension scheme started to wind up between 1ˢᵗ January 1997 to 5ᵗʰ April 2005.

- Pension Protection Fund (PPF). This scheme took over from the above to provide compensation where a scheme winds up on or after 6ᵗʰ April 2005 with too little in the fund or an insolvent employer. In general, compensation ensures that existing pensioners carry on getting the full amount of their pension and that other scheme members get 90% of their promised pension up to a maximum limit (£29,749 at 65 in 2010-11). The PPF is financed by a levy on occupational pension schemes.

## Protection of personal pensions

Nearly all personal pensions come under the umbrella of the Financial Services Authority (FSA). The FSA is a body with wide powers, given by parliament, and regulates a wide range of financial activities. In the United Kingdom, it is illegal to offer personal pensions without being authorized by the FSA. All pension providers authorized by then FSA have to go through a lot of hoops to demonstrate that they are responsible providers. The FSA oversees the activities of the Financial Services Compensation Scheme. If a firm providing personal pensions becomes insolvent the FSCS will step in and provide compensation instead. Compensation is capped at a maximum amount, which varies according to the way that your money has been invested. Currently the maximum is £50,000 for deposits, £50,000 for investments and for long term insurance (personal pensions, life insurance and annuities 90% of the claim with no upper limit).

## Complaining about pensions

### State pensions
In the first instance you would deal with HMRC, regarding payment of national insurance, and also the Pension Service regarding pension forecasts. You can find details about how to complain from HMRC website www.hmrc.gov.uk. If you have complained to the director of a particular office and you are not happy you can take your complaint to the Adjudicators Office (www.adjudicatorsoffice.gov.uk). This is an independent body that can deal with complaints about mistakes and delays, misleading advice and any other issue.

In the same way you should contact the Pensions Service department dealing with pension forecasts if you have a problem in this area. If the problem carries on without resolution you can contact the Pensions Service Chief Executive.

### Occupational schemes
You should initially contact the pension administrator for your scheme. If the problem is not resolved at this early stage then you should say that you want to use the formal complaints procedure, which all occupational schemes must have and must provide you with details of. If you receive no satisfaction with this process

then you should contact the Pensions Advisory Service (TPAS) www.pensionsadvisoryservice.org.uk.

TPAS is an independent mediation service which will help all parties reach agreement. If this doesn't work then you can go one step further and take your complaint to the Pensions Ombudsman. You must go through TPAS before the Ombudsman will consider your complaint.

## Personal pensions

You should complain first to the pensions provider. As mentioned, all firms authorized by the FSA must have a formal complaints procedure. Provided that you go down this route, and you are still unhappy, then you can complain to the Financial Ombudsman Service (FOS) www.financial-ombudsman.org.uk. It will investigate your complaint and can make orders which are binding on the firm. Where appropriate the FOS can make the firm pay you up to £100,000 to put the matter right.

# 15

## Options For Those Who Cannot Access an Occupational Scheme

If a person is self-employed, with an employer who does not run an occupational scheme, or eligible to join an occupational scheme, belongs to a group personal pension scheme, a stakeholder scheme or simply have not joined a scheme, for example run their own business and haven't got round to it, there are a number of options to consider.

For people who are self-employed, or in any of the situations mentioned above, it is quite often the case that it is difficult enough balancing the personal books without having to consider putting a monthly amount aside for a pension. However, it is crucial that this is done as time goes by and it is important to ensure that a pension is provided at the end of the working life.

The longer that pension contributions are delayed the more expensive that it become to make adequate provision.

\*\*\*\*\*\*\*\*\*\*\*\*

# 16

## Options for savings

### Personal pensions

We have discussed personal pensions as an option of saving for retirement. Savings are usually with an insurance company, through unit trusts. Banks and building societies can also offer these pension plans.

All personal pension plans operate on a money-purchase basis, basically the fund grows over time and provides a pension to the contributor. The drawback with money purchase schemes is that they offer no guarantees at all and depend very much on the performance of the stock market or other sectors of the economy. Therefore the pension at the end cannot be guaranteed. Another important factor is the annuity rate at the time of retirement (the amount of pension that the fund can buy).

### Qualifications for a personal pension

Nearly everyone under the age of 75 can qualify for a personal pension. The only people who cannot have a personal pension scheme are controlling directors who already belong to an occupational scheme and employees earning more than £30,000 a year who already belong to an occupational scheme.

With personal pension schemes, as with occupational schemes, a person can usually take a tax-free lump sum on retirement. This will reduce the amount of pension that a person gets. The amount of the lump sum will depend on the rules of the scheme.

A person doesn't have to stop work in order to take a pension from a personal plan. There are, as mentioned throughout this book, rules governing age that a person can take the pension. Usually, a person can start from 50 years of age upwards. People over 75 are prohibited from paying into a personal pension plan.

## What amounts to pay into a personal pension?

A person can make regular contributions on a monthly or annual basis or pay in a lump sum. Regular contributions can be increased. If the personal pension is a stakeholder scheme then the regular monthly contribution is limited to £20.

## Limits on what can be paid in

HMRC limits the amount of tax-free contributions that can be made. Nearly everyone can contribute £3,600 per annum in total to his or her scheme. This is the before-tax-relief (gross) contribution limit. Subtracting basic tax relief makes the limit £2,808 per year. If a person is earning the contributions can be more than this.

Earnings related contributions are set as a percentage of net relevant earnings. For an employee, this means total before tax pay, including the value of most fringe benefits. If a person is self-employed, net relevant earnings means profits for tax purposes. The limits indicate the maximum before-tax-relief amount that can be paid into a personal pension plan. The table overleaf shows the percentage contribution limits. In addition to the percentages listed overleaf there is an overall cash limit on the amount of earnings which can be taken into account in working out contribution limits.

Net relevant earnings used as a basis for contributions in any particular tax year do not have to be the earnings for that particular tax year. Net relevant earnings can be chosen from any of the previous five tax years as a basis for contributions. Anyone can pay contributions on behalf of the contributor, it doesn't have to be specifically the contributor.

## Tax relief limits on contributions to personal pensions

Age at the start of the tax year   Contribution limit as      Contribution

| Up to 35 | 17.5% | £175 |
| --- | --- | --- |
| 36-45 | 20% | £200 |
| 46-50 | 25% | £250 |
| 51-55 | 30% | £300 |
| 56-60 | 35% | £350 |
| 61-74 | 40% | £400 |
| 75 and over | No longer contribute | NLC |

## Tax relief on savings

A person will get tax relief up to the highest rate of income tax on the amount that is contributed to a personal pension. For example, a taxpayer paying tax at 22% can contribute £100 to a plan at a cost of only £78. A person will get basic-rate relief automatically by paying only the after-tax relief into the plan. A person will get this relief regardless of whether they pay tax or not. For the non-taxpayer, the relief is a bonus amount paid into the plan. If a contribution is paid towards someone else's pension plan basic rate tax relief is applicable. However, for higher rate taxpayer's no extra relief can be claimed on contributions into someone else's plan.

# 17

## Rules for Doctors and Dentists

GP's or dentists working in a practice are counted as self-employed for tax purposes. However, they are eligible to contribute to an occupational pension scheme-the National Health Service Superannuation Scheme. At the same time GP's and dentists can contribute to a personal pension scheme. A GP or dentist has a choice:

- Pay into the NHS scheme but give up all tax relief on these contributions. In this case all earnings count as net relevant earnings; the tax–relief for personal pension contributions or retirement annuity contributions is then worked out in the usual way.

- Pay into the NHS scheme and receive tax relief as normal on these contributions. Multiplying the NHS scheme contribution by 16 and two thirds gives a figure for earnings which are covered by the scheme. Subtracting this amount from total earnings leaves the amount of net relevant earnings which can be used as the basis of working out contributions to a personal pension scheme.

If a person belongs to the NHS scheme they can make Additional Voluntary Contributions (AVC's) as long as total contributions don't exceed the normal limit applying to an employers scheme which is 15% of earnings. AVC's can be made either to the NHS scheme or to a free-standing AVC scheme.

# 18

## Stakeholder Pension Schemes

In April 2001 the government introduced the stakeholder pension scheme. This type of scheme is not a new plan or scheme but a set of conditions that can be applied to either personal pensions or money purchase occupational schemes. If the conditions are met then the scheme can be called a 'stakeholder pension' and will represent good value for money.

The conditions that must be met are as follows:

- The scheme will have low charges, no more than 1.5% per annum
- Low and flexible contributions. Minimum of £20 per month
- Portable-can transfer out of one scheme into another without penalty
- Simplicity-the scheme must include a default investment option which determines how money is invested if individual doesn't choose an investment option for themselves
- Information-scheme provider to give benefit statement at least once per year

If the stakeholder scheme alters then the stakeholder must be informed.

Since October 2001, employers with more than five employees who do not offer a pension arrangement must give access to a stakeholder scheme through the workplace.

All stakeholder pensions operate on a money purchase basis. Like all other money purchase schemes the pension that you will get depends on amount paid into the scheme, tax relief, charges and how well the fund does.

# 19

## Choosing a Personal Pension Plan

---

There is a wide choice of personal pension schemes on offer. One common denominator is that the schemes are now heavily regulated by both the government and the Financial Services Authority. Most schemes will accept either a monthly contribution or a one-off lump sum payment per annum. The majority of schemes will allow a person to increase contributions. It is important to look for a plan that will allow a person to miss payments, in case of unemployment, sickness etc, without penalty.

### Investments

Plans which allow individuals to choose their own investments are called' Self-invested personal pensions' (SIIPS). A person will build up their own fund of personal investments from a wide range of options such as shares, gilts, property and other areas. However, unless an individual has a large sum to invest, this is unlikely to be a wise bet. Pension companies can offer their own expertise and usually have far greater knowledge than the individual.

### Unit trusts and unit-linked investments

These types of plans are offered by a lot of insurance companies. The money is allocated to units whose value is linked to a specific fund of investments. The return depends on the then price of the units. Like all investments, this value will rise and fall in line with the value of the underlying investment.

## Tracker funds

With a tracker fund, the main input from an investment manager is when the fund is first set up. The underlying investments are set to mimic a particular market as described by a given stock market index such as the FTSE 100. The fund is then left to track the market with no attempt being made by fund managers to switch to better markets. These types of funds do perform well and attract lower charges because of the lower input from fund managers.

## With-profits plans

These types of plans are, in the main, offered by insurance companies. Money is invested in a broad spread of investments. The return depends on how well the investments grow and also the provider's profits from other parts of its business. The return is in the form of bonuses, reversionary bonuses are added to the plan regularly. A terminal bonus is normally added on redemption. Statements are given to the pension holder showing how well the fund is doing, including an estimate of the terminal bonus. Be aware that this is only an estimate at a given time. It can rise or fall.

One disadvantage with this type of plan is that, if a person transfers their plan before it reaches maturity then any terminal bonus will be lost. Reversionary bonuses can also be lost. Therefore, when considering a with-profits plan it is very wise to read the small print.

## Funds that are bond-based

Bond-based funds are a particular type of unitised fund. In this case, the underlying investments are corporate bonds, preference shares and government bonds (gilts). They are known as fixed-interest investments.

A fund investing in bonds does not offer the same guaranteed returns, because fund managers will be buying and selling bonds all the time. Bonds are usually stable, particularly government bonds so the return can be expected to be stable also.

## Lifestyle investments

These are quite new and the overall investment plan is designed around a persons attitude towards risk and also the planned retirement date. The earlier that a person invests the more risk that may be taken and the later that investments occur the more cautious approach that may be adopted.

## Fees and other charges

Those who invest your money on your behalf don't work for nothing. Fees are charged. The rate of interest offered will reflect the ultimate charge and there will probably be an administration fee too. Some plans have very complicated charging structures and it is very important that these are understood before decisions are made.

## Other benefits from a personal pension

A personal pension scheme does not automatically offer a package of benefits in addition to the actual pension. Any additional benefits have to be paid for. The range of extra benefits includes lump sum life cover for dependants if death occurs before retirement, a pension for widow or widower or other partner, a waiver of contributions if there is an inability to work and a pension paid early if sickness or disability prevents working until retirement age.

A contracted out personal pension must allow for a widow's or widower's pension to be payable if the widow or widower is over 45 years of age, or is younger than 45 but qualifies for child benefit. The pension would be whatever amount can be bought by the fund built up through investing the contracting-out rebates. The widow or widower has an open market option, which gives him or her a right to shop around for a different pension provider rather than remain with the existing provider.

The pension could cease if the widow or widower remarries while under the state pension age, or ceases to be eligible for child benefit whilst still under 45. This depends on the terms of the contract at the time of death.

A contracted out widow's or widower's pension built up before 6th April 1997 must be increased each year in line with inflation, up to a maximum of 3% a year. For post April 1997 pensions this must be up to 5% per year and after 6th April 2005, pensions taken out don't have to increase at all.

With the exception of contracted out plans, a person must choose at the time of taking out the plan which death benefits to have as part of the scheme. Broadly, they should be in line with the benefits mentioned above.

### Retirement due to ill-health

If a person has to retire due to ill-health, a pension can be taken from a personal plan at any age. However, a person's inability to work must be clearly demonstrated and backed up with a professional opinion.

Taking a pension early will result in a reduced pension because what is in the pot will be less. However, there are ways of mitigating this, one way to ensure that a waiver of premiums in the event of sickness is included in the pension. In this way the plan will continue to grow even though a person is ill. Another way is to take out permanent disability insurance. This insurance will guarantee that the pension that you will get when you cannot work will at least be a minimum amount.

## The Pension Protection Fund
Members of defined benefit occupational pension schemes are protected through the PPF, which will pay regular compensation, based on your pension amount, if the company becomes insolvent and the pension scheme doesn't have enough money to pay your pension. The PPF applies to most defined benefit schemes where the employer became insolvent after 6th April 2005. You should check with the PPF about levels of compensation.

## The Financial Assistance Scheme
If you are an individual scheme member and have lost out on your pension as a result of your scheme winding up after 1st January 1997 and the introduction of PPF you may be able to get financial help from the FAS if:

- your defined benefit scheme was under funded and
- your employer is insolvent, no longer exists or has entered into a valid compromise agreement with the trustees of the pension fund to avoid insolvency; or
- in some circumstances, your final salary scheme was wound up because it could not pay members benefits even if the employer continues trading.

## In the case of fraud or theft

If the shortfall in your company pension scheme was due to fraud or theft, it may be possible to recover some of the money through the PPF who operate what is known as the Fraud Compensation Scheme.

## Closing a final salary scheme

If you belong to a final salary scheme, its trustees are responsible for making sure it doesn't run out of money. To limit future costs, the employer or the trustees can:

- 'close' the scheme to new members-meaning existing members can continue to contribute and receive a pension on retirement;
- 'freeze' the scheme-meaning the scheme is closed to everyone and existing members benefits stop building.

An employer (or the trustees) may decide to wind up a pension scheme at any time. This involves closing down the scheme to everyone and using its assets for the members benefit. If the company remains in business it at least has to provide access to a stakeholder scheme (to which they don't have to contribute) as a replacement.

## The Pension Tracing Service

If you think that you may have an old pension but are not sure of the details, the Pension Tracing Service may be able to help. They can be contacted on 0845 6002 537 and will give you full details of their scheme and also will tell you what they need from you in order to trace the pension.

# 20

## Tax and Pensions

### State pensions

State retirement pensions count as income for tax purposes. Tax may have to be paid if income received is high enough. The only exception to this is the £10 Christmas bonus paid to all pensioners.

State pension is paid without deduction of tax. This is convenient for non-taxpayers. For other taxpayers, the tax due will usually be deducted from PAYE or from any other pension that is received. If the tax is not deducted it will be collected through self-assessment in January and July instalments.

### Occupational schemes

A pension from an occupational scheme is treated as income for tax purposes. Usually, the pension will be paid with tax deducted through the PAYE system, along with any other tax due.

### Personal pensions

A personal pension will count as income for tax purposes. The pension provider will usually deduct tax through PAYE. Likewise, any other tax due will be deducted through the PAYE system. The local tax office should be contacted in order to determine individual tax positions.

### Tax in retirement

When a person retires, their tax bill continues to be worked out in the usual way. However, higher tax allowances may apply so less tax is paid. The calculations used to work out a person's individual tax bill are as follows:

- Income from all sources is added together. This includes all income with the exception of income that is tax-free.

- Outgoings that you pay in full are deducted from taxable income. 'Outgoings' means any expenditure that qualifies for tax relief.

- Allowances are subtracted. Everyone has a personal allowance. For current allowances, contact the local HMRC Office or Citizens Advice Bureau. There is a breakdown below

- What is left is taxable income. This divided into four. The first slice 10% is paid (0-£2560) the second slice tax is paid at the basic rate (0-£35,500) the third slice 35,001-150,000 is subject to 40% tax. The fourth slice is over 150,000 subject to 50% tax. (as at 2011/2012)

- Married couples allowance-this is a reduced rate allowance, given at a rate of 10% as a reduction to a person's tax bill. Married couples allowance is given only where a husband or wife were born before 6th April 1935.

## Tax allowances for retirees

In the tax year 2011/12 the basic personal allowance for most people is £7,475. However, if a person is 65 or over at any time during a tax year, there will be a higher personal allowance, the age-allowance. There are two rates of age allowance: in the 2008/9 tax year the allowance is £9940 for people reaching ages

65 to 74, and the higher age allowance is £10090 for people reaching ages 75 or more.

A husband and wife can each get a personal allowance to set against their own income. There is an extra allowance called a married couples allowance if either husband or wife, or both, were born before 6th April 1935. In 2011/12 this is £7295 if the couple are aged over 75. The allowance doesn't apply to those under 75.

While the personal allowance saves tax at the highest rate, the married couples allowance only gives tax relief at the rate of 10% in the 2011/12tax year. If the husbands income is above a certain level then the married couples allowance is reduced, but never to less than a basic amount. A wife can elect to have half the basic amount of the married couples allowance (but not any of the age-related addition) set against her own income. Alternatively, the husband and wife can elect jointly for the whole basic amount to be transferred to the wife.

### Income limit for age allowance
Age allowances are reduced for people with earnings above a certain level. The personal age allowance is reduced if a person has a total income of more than £24,000 in the tax year 2011/12. The married couple's age allowance is also reduced if this is the case. In either case, the reduction is £1 for every £2 over the limit. Where the husband is receiving both age-related personal allowance and age-related married couple's allowance, his personal allowance is reduced first and then the married couple's allowance. The reduction stops once the allowances fall to a basic amount.

# 21

## Reaching Retirement Age

On reaching retirement age, it will be necessary to ensure that all paperwork relating to pension contributions is in order. There are a number of rules that should be observed in order to ensure that any pension due is paid:

- keep all documents relating to pension rights
- start organising any pension due before retirement, this will ensure that any problems are overcome well before retirement

It is very important that communication is kept with all pension providers, and that they have accurate up-to-date records of a person's whereabouts. Each time addresses are changed this should be communicated to all pension providers. If it is impossible to track down an old employer from whom a pension is due, the Pension Schemes Registry can help. This was set up in 1990, by the government to help people trace so-called 'lost pensions'. If help is needed this can be obtained by filling in form PR4 which can be obtained from the Pensions Advisory Service or the Pensions Scheme Registry.

### How to claim state pension

A letter will be sent to all retiree's about four months before retirement date. This will come from the pension service and will detail how much pension is due. The pension is not paid automatically, it has to be claimed. This can be done by phoning the Pensions Claim Line number included with the letter, or by filling in a claim form BR1. If the person is a married man and the wife is claiming based on the husbands contributions, then form BF225 should be filled in.

If the pension is to be deferred it is advisable to contact the Pensions Service in writing as soon as possible.

A late pension claim can be backdated up to twelve months. If a man is claiming for a pension for his wife based on his contributions this can only be backdated six-months.

### How the pension is paid
Pensions are paid by the DWP pension direct to a bank account or Post Office Card Account. To find out more about the payment of pensions contact the DWP Direct Payment Information Line.

### Leaving the country
If a person goes abroad for less than six months, they can carry on receiving pension in the normal way. If the trip is for longer then the Pension Service should be contacted and one of the following arrangements can be made to pay a pension:

- Have it paid into a personal bank account while away

- Arrange for it to be paid into a Post Office Card Account

- Arrange for the money to be paid abroad

If a person is living outside of the UK at the time of the annual pension increase they won't qualify for the increase unless they reside in a member country of the European Union or a country with which the UK has an agreement for increasing pensions. It is very important that you check what will happen to your state pension when you move abroad. The DWP International Pension Centre can help.

## Pensions from an occupational scheme

Although different schemes have different arrangements, there are similar rules for each scheme. About three months before a person reaches normal retirement age, they should contact the scheme. Either telephone or write enclosing all the details that they will need. The following questions should be asked:

- What pension is due?

- What is the lump-sum entitlement?

- How will the pension be reduced if a lump sum is taken?

- How will the pension be paid, will there be any choices as to frequency?

- Is there a widow's or widowers pension, and if so how will it affect the retirement pension?

- Are there any pensions for other dependants in the event of death?

If a person has been making Additional Voluntary Contributions, then a detailed breakdown of these will be needed.

# Retiring early

Retirement earlier than the normal age for a scheme may result in payment of a pension at an earlier age. The minimum age for a pension is 50 with the exception of retirement on ill-health grounds. A scheme administrator will be able to supply full details.

# Retiring late

Depending on the rules of the occupational scheme it may be possible to delay retirement and take the pension later. Again, the scheme administrators can help.

# Method of payment

Depending on how the pension is arranged, it may be paid direct from the provider or via an insurance company. The usual for pension payments is either quarterly or monthly in advance into a personal bank account. The scheme administrators will be able to provide more information with regard to this.

# A pension from a personal plan

In the same way as a pension from an occupational scheme, it is necessary to get in touch with the pension provider about 3-4 months before retirement date. The main questions that should be asked are:

- How much is the pension fund worth?

- How much pension will the plan provider offer?

- Can an increase be arranged each year and if so how much is the increase?

- What is the maximum lump sum?

- Is there a widow's or widowers or other dependants pension?

- What are the other options if any?

- Can the purchase of an annuity be deferred without affecting the drawing of an income?

Pensions can only be paid by an insurance company or a friendly society so if the pension has been with any other form of provider then it has to be switched before it can be paid.

If there are protected-rights from a contracted out pension plan, these can be, may have to be, treated quite separately from the rest of a pension. Protected rights from a personal pension cannot be paid until a person has reached 60 years of age. A person must, by law, have an open market option enabling protected rights pension to be paid by another provider, if it is desired.

## Choosing the right annuity

It is very important that an open market option is exercised at retirement. Advice should be obtained from a specialist annuity advisor. If husband and wife, it may be advisable to take out a joint annuity which will carry on paying out an income until the last partner dies, otherwise a widower or widow could be left in financial hardship.

One popular option is an annuity that pays a guaranteed income for five-years. The usual annuity pays a lifetime income then stops on death. Another option is to take out an increasing annuity. This is compulsory for contracted-out pension rights, but otherwise optional.

As annuities have fallen over the years, another option is to take out a with-profits annuity. This is a higher risk option but offers a higher return. Income from a with-profits annuity is usually made up of two parts: a guaranteed basic payment and bonuses. At the time of taking out the annuity a person must choose the starting income which the annuity will provide. The choice will depend on the likely level of future bonuses (assumed bonuses ABR) and the degree of risk that can be borne. There is a choice between:

- Low ABR (minimum 0% or no bonuses). The annuity income will start at a very low level. But as long as any bonus is declared the income will increase.

- Higher ABR (maximum say 4%). The starting income will be higher. The higher the ABR that is chosen the greater the starting income. Each year, provided the bonus that is declared is greater than the ABR that you chose, the income will increase. If the declared bonus is lower than the ABR, the income will fall back.

### Annuity deferral and income withdrawal

Pension plans set up on or after 1st May 1995 can offer the option of annuity deferral and income withdrawal which allows a person to start taking an income from a pension plan but without buying an annuity. Instead, the income is drawn down direct from the pension fund. The remaining fund must be used to buy an annuity before the age of 75. The income must be reviewed every three years to ensure that the pension fund isn't being depleted too fast.

## Payments of personal pensions

If the amount involved is very small then this can be taken as a lump sum. The amount is £2,500 or less or is too small to buy a £250 annuity income. Otherwise, the usual arrangements will apply, with you choosing the most convenient method of payment, by cheque, or payment monthly or quarterly into a bank account.

# Useful Addresses

## Association of Consulting Actuaries
1 Wardrobe Place
London EC4V 5AG
020 7248 3163
www.aca.org.uk

Association of Chartered Certified Accountants
29 Lincolns Inn Field
London WC2A 3EE
020 7059 5000
www.acca.co.uk

## Department for Work and Pensions (DWP)
Caxton House
Tothill Street
London SW1H 9DA
DWP Direct Payment Information line
0800 107 2000
www.dwp.gov.uk/directpayment

DWP Public Enquiry Office
020 7712 2171
www.dwp.gov.uk

Financial Services Authority (FSA)
25 The North Colonnade
Canary Wharf
London E14 5HS

Consumer Helpline 0845 606 1234

www.fas.gov.uk
FSA Comparative Tables 0845 606 1234
www.fas.gov.uk/tables
FSA Register 0845 606 1234
www.fsa.gov.uk/consumer

Financial Services Compensation Scheme
7th Floor
Lloyds Chambers
Portsoken Street
London E1 8BN
020 7892 7300
www.fscs.org.uk

Financial Ombudsman Service
South Quay Plaza
183 Marsh Wall
London E14 9SR
0800 0234 567
www.financialombudsman.org.uk

HMRC
For local tax enquiries look in phone book under HMRC
Or go to
www.hmrc.gov.uk

Institute of Chartered Accountants in England and Wales
Chartered Accountants Hall
PO Box 433 Moorgate Place
London EC2P 2BJ
020 7920 8100
www.icaew.co.uk

Institute of Chartered Accountants in Ireland
Chartered Accountants House
83 Pembroke Road
Dublin 4
Republic of Ireland
00 353 1 668 0842
www.icai.ie

Institute of Chartered Accountants in Scotland
CA House
21 Haymarket Yard
Edinburgh EH12 5BH
0131 347 0100
www.icas.org.uk

Institute of Actuaries
Staple Inn
High Holborn
London WC1V 7QJ
020 7632 2100
www.actuaries.org.uk

Institute of Financial Planning
Whitefriars Centre
Lewins Mead
Bristol BS1 2NT
0117 9345 2470
www.financialplaning.org.uk

International Pension Centre
Tyneview Park Newcastle Upon Tyne NE98 1BA
0191 218 7777

Occupational Pensions Regulatory Authority
Invicta House
Trafalgar Place
Brighton BN1 4DW
01273 627600
www.opra.gov.uk

Pensions Advisory Service
11 Belgrave Road
London SW1V 1RB
0845 601 2923
www.pensionsadvisoryservice.org.uk

Pensions Ombudsman
Same as above
www. pensions-ombudsman.org.uk

Pensions Protection Fund
Knollys House
17 Addiscombe Road
Croydon
Surrey
CRO 6SR
0845 600 2541
www.pensionprotectionfund.org.uk

Pension Tracing Service
The Pension Service
Tyneview Park
Whitley Road
Newcastle Upon Tyne
NE98 1BA

0845 6002 537
www.thepensionservice.gov.uk

Pension Schemes Registry
PO box 133
Newcastle Upon Tyne
NE99 1NN
0191 225 6316
www.opra.gov.uk/traceAPension

Pension Service (The)
Pensions Information line 0845 31 32 33
Pensions Forecasting Service 0845 3000 168
Pension Credit Application Line 0800 99 1234
www.thepensionservice.gov.uk

Society of Pension Consultants
St Bartholomew House
92 Fleet Street
London EC4Y 1DG
020 7353 1688
www.spc.uk.com

Index

Straightforward Guides

Buy online, using credit card or other forms of payment by going to www.straightfowardco.co.uk A discount of 25% per title is offered with online purchases.

**Law**
*A Straightforward Guide to:*
Consumer Rights
Bankruptcy Insolvency and the Law
Employment Law
Private Tenants Rights
Family law
Small Claims in the County Court
Contract law
Intellectual Property and the law
Divorce and the law
Leaseholders Rights
The Process of Conveyancing
Knowing Your Rights and Using the Courts
Producing Your own Will
Housing Rights
The Bailiff the law and You
Probate and The Law
Company law
What to Expect When You Go to Court
Guide to Competition Law
Give me Your Money-Guide to Effective Debt Collection
Caring for a Disabled Child

## General titles

Letting Property for Profit
Buying, Selling and Renting property
Buying a Home in England and France
Bookkeeping and Accounts for Small Business
Understanding the Stock market
Creative Writing
Freelance Writing
Writing Your own Life Story
Writing performance Poetry
Writing Romantic Fiction
Speech Writing

Teaching Your Child to Read and write
Teaching Your Child to Swim
Raising a Child-The Early Years
Creating a Successful Commercial Website
The Straightforward Business Plan
The Straightforward C.V.
Successful Public Speaking
Handling Bereavement
Play the Game-A Compendium of Rules
Individual and Personal Finance
Understanding Mental Illness
The Two-Minute Message
Guide to Self Defence
Buying a Used Car
Tiling for Beginners

Go to:

www.straightforwardco.co.uk